LEGENDARY HEROES
OF THE WILD WEST

KIT
CARSON
FRONTIER SCOUT

**William R. Sanford &
Carl R. Green**

ENSLOW PUBLISHERS, INC.
44 Fadem Road   P.O. Box 38
Box 699   Aldershot
Springfield, N.J. 07081 Hants GU12 6BP
U.S.A.   U.K.

Library of Congress Cataloging-in-Publication Data

Sanford, William R. (William Reynolds), 1927–
    Kit Carson: frontier scout / William R. Sanford and Carl R. Green.
        p. cm. — (Legendary Heroes of the Wild West)
    Summary: The life of Kit Carson, legendary scout, mountain man,
and Indian fighter of the Old West.
    ISBN 0-89490-650-X
    1. Carson, Kit, 1809–1868—Juvenile literature. 2. Pioneers—West
(U.S.)—Biography—Juvenile literature. 3. Scouts and scouting—
West (U.S.)—Biography—Juvenile literature. 4. Soldiers—West
(U.S.)—Biography—Juvenile literature. 5. West (U.S.)—Biography—
Juvenile literature. [1. Carson, Kit, 1809–1868. 2. Pioneers.
3. West (U.S.)—Biography.] I. Green, Carl R. II. Title.
III. Series: Sanford, William R. (William Reynolds), 1927–
Legendary heroes of the Wild West.
F592.C33S25 1996
978'.02'092—dc20
[B]   95-36838
                                            CIP
                                            AC

Printed in the United States of America

10 9 8 7 6 5 4 3 2 1

Illustration Credits: Kit Carson Historic Museums, Taos, New Mexico,
pp. 6, 12, 25, 28, 30, 32, 33, 38, 40, 41; William R. Sanford and Carl R.
Green, pp. 7, 11, 15, 16, 19, 21, 24, 36.

Cover Illustration: Paul Daly

CONTENTS

AUTHORS' NOTE

This book tells the true story of Kit Carson. Kit was one of the Wild West's greatest heroes. In his day, he was known as an outstanding scout, mountain man, and Indian fighter. His skill, bravery, and daring exploits were featured in newspapers, magazines, and dime novels. In more recent years, Kit has been featured in novels, films, and biographies. You may be amazed that one man could pack so much adventure into a single lifetime. If so, rest easy. All of the events described in this book really happened.

1
CROSSING THE SIERRA NEVADA

In the early 1840s, much of the West was still unexplored. John Charles Frémont and Kit Carson took on the task of mapping the vast region. Frémont was on his way to becoming the foremost explorer of his day. Kit was a little known scout and mountain man. That changed when Frémont's reports reached the public. The stories of Kit's skill and courage turned him into a national hero.

Late in 1843, Kit was Frémont's guide on a trip to Oregon country. By year's end the expedition had turned south. The route pointed toward the eastern Sierra Nevada in present-day Nevada, and led into the Great Basin. A search for the fabled Buenaventura River drew a blank. No such river flowed through the mountains to the West Coast. Christmas brought little cheer. A small ration of brandy could not drive out the chill.

In mid-January Frémont held a council. The party

Kit Carson belonged to that tough, resourceful breed known as mountain men. He gained his first fame by leading John C. Frémont on an "impossible" crossing of the Sierra Nevada during the winter of 1843–1844. In this engraving the artist posed Kit with his favorite horse, Apache.

could not turn east, Frémont said. That route led over jagged rocks that would cripple their mules. If they stayed where they were, they would starve or be killed by warlike Native Americans. The smoke of signal fires already rose from the nearby heights. Their best bet was to head west toward California.[1] Frémont counted on Kit to find a way through the Sierras.

Every mile was a struggle. At night, the temperature dropped to –19° C (–2° F). Mountain streams froze over. The men had to break the ice so the mules could drink. Native Americans appeared, eager to trade pine nuts for mirrors and beads. Asked to serve as guides, they told Kit to wait for spring. No one can cross the mountains in winter, they warned.[2]

Kit roused the sleeping camp at 3 A.M. each day. The early start allowed the pack train to plod forward on hard-crusted snow. The men wore crude snowshoes. As the day wore on, the crust softened. Horses and mules would flounder in deep snow. Kit's work crew beat the snow with mallets to make a usable trail. Frémont had hauled a small cannon all the way from St. Louis. Now he left it behind in a snowbank.

Animals and men went hungry. The starving mules chewed on their harness. When a mule died, the men dined on the carcass. At one point, Frémont allowed the cook to grill the party's dog. The menu that night featured "pea soup, mule, and dog."[3]

Kit did his best to keep spirits high. He told the men, "Thar over the ridge lies the purtiest valley in the world. . . . I know it, 'cause I war thar fifteen years ago."[4] The climb took the expedition through a pass at 9,338 feet. Frémont named it Carson Pass in honor of his guide. On February 1, Kit spotted a range of mountains that he knew. Two more weeks, he told Frémont, would take them to the Sacramento Valley.

Kit led the way down steep hillsides to a shallow stream. Always sure-footed, he jumped across.

Once it left civilization behind, a survey party had to be self-supporting. Horses and mules carried the supplies and equipment. Bogged down in deep snow while crossing high mountain passes, starving men sometimes ate their pack animals.

Frémont was not as agile. His moccasins slipped, and he fell into the icy water. Thinking Frémont was hurt, Kit jumped in to rescue him. After both men regained their footing, they searched in vain for Frémont's rifle. At last, chilled to the bone, they climbed out. Kit built a fire to drive out the damp and the cold.[5]

The weary men rejoiced when they reached the valley floor. The weakest men and animals stayed there to rest. Kit led Frémont and the others to Sutter's Fort on the Sacramento River. On March 6, Captain Sutter rode out to greet the weary explorers. They were the first, he told them, to cross the Sierra Nevada in midwinter.

Perhaps Sutter should not have been surprised. Kit Carson was one of the greatest mountain men who ever lived.

2
A FRONTIER CHILDHOOD

Christopher Houston Carson was born in Kentucky on Christmas Eve, 1809. Right from birth he was called Kit. His mother Rebecca was Lindsey Carson's second wife. Lindsey's first wife, Lucy, had five children before she died. Rebecca had ten more.

The Carsons lived in a log cabin warmed by a huge fireplace. The main room served as kitchen, dining, and living room. The children climbed a ladder to their beds in a sleeping loft. Travelers from the West sometimes bedded down near the fireplace. They paid for their suppers with tales of cheap land and high adventure.

In 1811 the Carsons joined the westward movement. Lindsey settled in Howard County, Missouri. This was frontier country. When the Native Americans went on the warpath, the settlers crowded into crude forts. Life was hard, but few complained. As one settler wrote, "No man owing a dollar, no taxes to pay, we lived happy and prosperous . . ."[1]

Kit was small, with wavy blond hair that fell across a high forehead. Like most boys, he loved to hunt and fish. Unlike his friends, he studied the local Native Americans. The knowledge he gained came in handy all through his life.

Kit's father saw that his son had a quick mind. Maybe the boy would grow up to be a lawyer. The dream vanished the year Kit was eight. Lindsey was clearing his land when a tree limb fell and killed him. With his father dead, Kit had to quit school. Later, he often joked about his three years in the classroom. As he told a friend, "I was a young boy in the school house when the cry came, 'Indians!' I jumped to my rifle and threw down my spelling book, and there it lies."[2]

Four years later Kit's mother married Joseph Martin. Like many teenagers, Kit was hard to control. When he was fourteen, Martin put him to work in a saddle-maker's shop owned by David Workman. Workman treated Kit fairly, but the boy yearned for the outdoor life.

Mountain men sometimes stopped at Workman's shop. The more stories they told, the more Kit hated his workbench. At last, in August 1826, Kit ran away. Workman followed custom by running an ad serving notice of Kit's flight. In his heart, he must have wished his apprentice well. To make sure no one brought the boy back, he offered only a one cent reward.[3]

A wagon train was about to leave for Santa Fe. Kit showed up, rifle in hand, and asked for a job. Captain Charles Bent, the wagon master, liked his looks. He hired the boy as herder and saddle mender. Along the trail, Kit learned about prairie fires and buffalo stampedes. He killed rattlesnakes and heard wolves howling. Native American raiding parties were the greatest threat. At night the men kept the stock inside a circle of wagons.

In the 1820s, Santa Fe still belonged to Mexico. That did not stop a crowd from greeting the Americans. News and trade goods from the east were rare in New Mexico. Kit picked up his wages from Bent—ten dollars, a blanket, and a tin cup. Santa Fe, he found, was too tame. He joined a party headed for Taos, New Mexico.

In Taos, gunsmith Matthew Kincaid gave the boy a place to stay. Kit soon picked up Spanish and

~~~~~~~~~~~~~~~~~~~~~~

At age sixteen, Kit ran away from his boring job as apprentice to a saddler. Luckily, David Workman was a friend as well as a boss. Workman ran this notice in the local newspaper as required by a law relating to runaway apprentices. As he must have planned, the one-cent reward did not set off a widespread search for the teenager.

Notice is hereby given to all persons,
THAT CHRISTOPHER CARSON, a boy about 16 years old, small of his age, but thick set; light hair, ran away from the subscriber, living in Franklin, Howard county, Missouri, to whom he had been bound to learn the saddler's trade, on or about the first of September last. He is supposed to have made his way towards the upper part of the state. All persons are notified not to harbor, support or assist said boy under the penalty of the law. One cent reward will be given to any person who will bring back the said boy.
DAVID WORKMAN.
Franklin, Oct. 6, 1826   16-3

several Native American languages. He also learned sign language. Kincaid taught Kit how to repair guns and to read trail signs. Together, they trapped beaver and hunted buffalo. Kit used the hides to make his own fringed shirts and pants.

Kit wanted to join the trappers who used Taos as a base. They laughed and told him, "You're too small, too young, too green."[4] In the spring of 1827, he signed on with an eastbound caravan. On the trail, he met some trappers heading west. They talked Kit into turning back. That summer he earned $1 a day as a wagon driver.

When fall came, Kit returned to Taos. Storekeeper Ewing Young hired him as a cook. All that winter, he listened spellbound as the trappers spun tall tales. Someday, Kit promised himself, he would be one of them.

Dressed in style for a visit to Washington, D.C., a stern-faced Kit Carson posed for this portrait around 1848. Some experts believe this may be the first photo ever taken of the famous mountain man.

3

"WE PASSED THE TIME GLORIOUSLY"

❦❦❦❦❦❦❦❦

Kit liked Taos, but he had not come west to be a cook. In the spring of 1828, he hooked up with a wagon train heading south. Kit's command of Spanish earned him the job. The trail to Chihuahua crossed five hundred miles of desert. It was marked by the half-buried skeletons of men, horses, and oxen.

That winter Kit took a job at a Mexican copper mine. He soon tired of driving ore wagons and headed back to Taos. He was twenty now, and he had grown two inches. He stood 5 feet 7 inches and weighed 160 pounds. Even though he was small and shy, he could hold his own in a fight.

In August 1829, Ewing Young chose Kit to join a fur-trapping expedition. Kit left Taos on horseback, a long-barreled rifle cradled in one arm. His saddlebag held powder and shot, spare moccasins, and a blanket. A pouch hung around his neck. It contained tobacco, flint and steel, and a pipe.[1]

One night Young saw a band of Apache sneaking toward the camp. He guessed the raiders planned to steal some horses. Thinking fast, Young ordered Kit and the others to hide. The Apache, seeing only a few white men, attacked. As they stormed into the camp, the hidden trappers opened fire. At least fifteen Apache died in the ambush. The rest of the band fled. That night, Kit drove a brass tack into the stock of his rifle. The tack marked his first life-or-death fight.[2]

By day the trappers worked the Salt and Gila rivers. The harvest of beaver furs grew daily. At night the Apache took their revenge. In ones and twos, they crept into camp to steal supplies and kill horses. Careless trappers, Kit learned, did not live long.

The growing load of furs slowed progress. Young solved the problem by sending some of his men back to Taos with the furs. The rest of us, Young said, are going to California. Before starting out, the men made "water tanks" of deer hide. The extra water did not last long in the desert heat. Four days out, thirsty mules led the men to a waterhole. Another four throat-parching days took the party to the Colorado River. That night the trappers feasted on a mare Young bought from a Mojave village. Three days later the trappers crossed the river on reed rafts.

A well-marked trail led to San Gabriel Mission near Los Angeles. Kit rejoiced at the sight of fields of grapes,

Kit Carson joined his first fur-trapping expedition in 1829. He developed into a skillful hunter, trapper, and guide in the months that followed. The young mountain man also proved his coolness under fire when Apache raiders attacked his camp.

corn, and wheat. He described the mission as "a paradise on earth."[3] From San Gabriel, the trappers moved northward. Kit memorized the route. When he met fellow trappers, he asked them to describe the land ahead. Each answer added to the map he kept in his head.

That summer, priests at San José Mission asked Young for help. Some Native Americans who had been forced to work at the mission had run away. Kit helped track the runaways to their village. The twelve mountain men then captured the village and burned it. A day later they returned the runaways to the mission. In the meantime, Native Americans had driven off sixty of Young's horses.

Kit and his mountain men tracked the thieves deep into the mountains. The chase ended at the raiders' camp. There, Kit led a surprise attack that recaptured fifty-four horses. The thieves had eaten the other six.[4]

That fall the trappers retraced their steps. In Los Angeles, Young's lack of a trapping license nearly led to disaster. Fearing arrest by Mexican officials, Young sent Kit ahead with the furs and extra horses. The rest of the party stayed to sample the free liquor offered by the officials. The plan was to arrest the trappers when they were too drunk to resist. When the time came, the plan

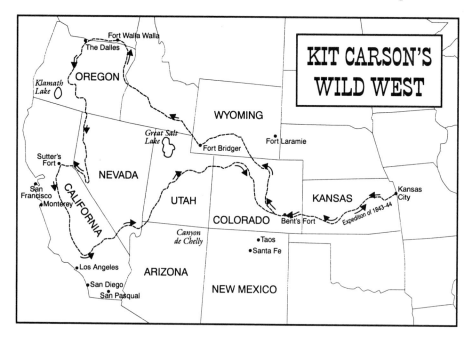

Born in Kentucky, Kit Carson spent most of his adventurous life in the Southwest. He lived in Taos, New Mexico, but he was most at home in the wilderness. His expeditions with John C. Frémont opened up vast new areas of the West to settlement.

was scratched. No one wanted the job of trying to arrest the well-armed trappers.

In April 1831, the three-year adventure ended. The trappers sold their furs in Santa Fe for $12 a pound. Kit's share did not last long. He later wrote, "We passed the time gloriously, spending the money freely, never thinking that our lives had been risked in gaining it."[5]

4

THE LIFE OF A MOUNTAIN MAN

Five months later Kit's money was gone. It was time to go back to work. In September 1831, he signed on with the Rocky Mountain Fur Company. The company furnished him with a mule, saddle, traps, and supplies. Kit repaid the loan with 104 prime beaver skins.[1]

For the next ten years, Kit lived in the Rockies. He and his fellow mountain men set traps along the Platte, Sweetwater, and Green rivers. There were swift streams to ford and grizzly bears to avoid. The greatest danger came from Native Americans. The Blackfoot and Crow tribes hunted in the region. Horse stealing was part of their way of life.

In one incident, a band of Crow stole nine horses. Kit and his fellow trappers needed the horses to carry supplies and furs. The next day Kit led eleven trappers on a forty-mile pursuit. At last they spotted a campfire. Outnumbered five-to-one, Kit gambled on a bold plan. That night he and five men crawled close to the Crow camp. There they cut the horses free and drove them to their own camp. Leaving three men on guard, the others crept back to where the Crow lay sleeping. This time a barking dog awoke the camp. The trappers shot several warriors as they scrambled for cover.[2]

The mountain men lived by the changing seasons.

Horse stealing was a way of life for Native Americans in the 1800s. Kit Carson and his fellow mountain men kept a sharp lookout for Crow, Blackfoot, and Apache raiders. A long chase and a fierce gun battle often followed a raid like the one pictured in this old engraving.

When the weather turned cold, they moved into a winter camp. It was a time for playing cards and racing horses. If someone had a book, he read aloud to the others. There was work to do, too. Kit helped cut timber to build snug cabins. When meat ran short, he hunted deer in the nearby woods. Like the others, he kept what he needed and shared the rest.

By April Kit and the other trappers were back in the mountains. If beaver were plentiful, they would collect hundreds of pelts. To keep the furs safe, Kit buried them in a cache. As the weather warmed up, the beavers shed their thick winter fur. That ended the trapping season, because summer pelts were worthless. With horses piled high with furs, Kit and his friends would head for a rendezvous. There they met traders who bought the furs for eastern hatmakers. The traders paid $3.75 for a typical pelt. With money in hand, the trappers drank, smoked, and gambled. When sober, they bought supplies for the coming year. A bar of lead for making bullets cost $1. Sugar, coffee, and gunpowder sold for $2 a pint. A wool blanket could cost eight good pelts.[3]

In 1835 Kit found a wife at the rendezvous. She was an Arapaho named Waanibe (Grass Singing). Kit called her Alice. Because Waanibe was young and pretty, her bride price was high. Kit paid her father a new gun, three mules, and five blankets.[4] Two years later Waanibe gave birth to a baby girl. Kit named her Adaline, after his niece. He grieved when Waanibe died of fever in 1838. Kit could not take Adaline on his trapping trips. He left her at Bent's

A fur trapper on his way to a rendezvous slips past a hostile Native American village. After months of trapping along remote mountain streams, mountain men looked forward to the lively social life at the rendezvous. Kit Carson met his first wife at one of these gatherings.

Fort in Colorado. A Native American woman took care of her.

Silk hats became the new fashion rage in 1841. Worse yet, overtrapping made beaver scarce. The price fell to $1 a pelt. Kit put away his traps and took a job as a hunter for Bent's Fort. In 1841 his pay of $1 a day supported father and daughter. Tough, straight-shooting men signed up to hunt with him. Before long they were calling themselves Carson Men.

Kit took a new wife that year, a Cheyenne named Making-Out-Road. The marriage did not last. The young woman did not like being a stepmother. Kit thought she worked too little and spent too much on beads. After a stormy argument, Making-Out-Road threw Kit's clothes out of their lodge. It was a divorce, Cheyenne-style.[5]

The record shows that Kit was not too upset. He gathered his gear and rode back to Taos. A girl named Josefa Jaramillo was waiting there.

5

ON THE TRAIL WITH FRÉMONT

❦

Kit did not want his daughter to grow up in the mountains. In April 1842, he took Adaline to St. Louis to go to school. His sister, Mary Ann Rubey, made the girl feel welcome.

To escape the crowded town, Kit took a steamboat up the Missouri. On board he met Lieutenant John Frémont, who would one day be called the Pathfinder. The young explorer liked Kit's steady gaze and frank speech. He hired the mountain man to guide him to the Rockies. The pay was $100 a month. That was three times Kit's pay as a hunter.[1]

The party reached the Kansas River in mid-June. Frémont had designed a rubber boat to ferry supplies. On the last trip, the overloaded boat capsized. Some boxes floated, others sank. Kit and his friend Lucien Maxwell dived in and saved most of the cargo.

The trip had its share of humor, too. One day Henry Brant galloped back from a morning ride. A scalping party was lurking nearby, the teenager shouted. Kit saddled up and rode out to scout the danger. Minutes later he came back laughing. Henry's "war party," he said, had turned out to be a herd of elk.[2]

On the way to Fort Laramie, the party met Jim Bridger. The famous mountain man warned that the Sioux were on the warpath. The news alarmed the greenhorns in the group. Kit and Frémont ignored their fears and pressed on. The Sioux did not attack. Frémont had convinced their chiefs that the army would punish them if they killed him.

The route along the North Platte took the party to

Life in the Wild West was seldom peaceful. In this old engraving, a band of Sioux are attacking Fort Union in Dakota Territory. John C. Frémont used some fast talk to prevent a similar attack near Fort Laramie. He convinced the Sioux war chiefs that the U.S. Army would punish them if they killed him and his men.

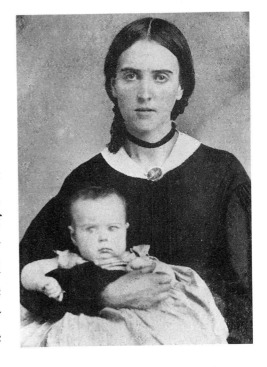

After two marriages to Native American women, Kit Carson married Josefa Jaramillo. Josefa made a home for her footloose husband in Taos, New Mexico.

South Pass. From there Kit guided Frémont and a dozen men to the top of Gannet Peak in present-day Wyoming. Frémont planted an American flag there. The job done, Kit led the way back to Fort Laramie. He had business in Taos.

Josefa Jaramillo welcomed him home. Lewis Garrard, who knew her, envied Kit. "Her beauty," he wrote, "was . . . such as would lead a man . . . to risk his life for one smile."[3] After Kit and Josefa wed in February 1843, they lived in Taos. To earn money, Kit carried mail between Taos and Bent's Fort in Colorado.

In July 1843, Frémont asked Kit to rejoin him. On this journey, Frémont's orders sent them west along the Oregon Trail. After a detour to the Great Salt Lake, the party pushed northwest. From Walla Walla, Kit followed the south bank of the Columbia River. On November 4, the party reached the Dalles. There the great river churned and whirled as it flowed between narrow cliffs. It was an awesome sight.

From the Dalles, Kit led the way south through the Great Basin. Two months later the men set up camp near present-day Reno, Nevada. It was there that Frémont asked Kit to guide him across the Sierra Nevada. Once he reached Sutter's Fort, Kit was on ground he knew. The return journey on the Old Spanish Trail went smoothly.

To please Josefa, Kit bought a farm near Taos. With Lucien Maxwell as his partner, he built fences, planted crops, and herded cattle. The quiet life ended in August 1845. Kit heard that Frémont was planning a third expedition. He sold the farm at a loss and rode to join his friend. Frémont wrote, "This was like Carson, prompt, self-sacrificing, and true."[4]

By February 1846, Kit and Frémont were back in California. The mood there was tense. A war was about to break out between Mexico and the United States. Mexican officials ordered Frémont to leave. The party moved on to Oregon, where the men had to fight for their lives. A band of Klamath warriors attacked on a night Frémont failed to post a guard. In the midst of the struggle, Kit tackled the Klamath war chief. As the two men fought, a mountain man shot the chief. With their leader dead, the war party withdrew.

Frémont ordered his men to march south. He was spurred by a message from his father-in-law, Senator Thomas Hart Benton of Missouri. If war comes, your place is in California, Benton had written. Frémont agreed. Someone should be there to raise the Stars and Stripes.[5]

6

A MOUNTAIN MAN TURNS SOLDIER

In 1846 California was a hotbed of rebellion. American settlers wanted to detach the province from Mexico. Wealthy Mexicans (the Californios) feared the loss of their ranches if the United States took control. Offshore, British warships lay at anchor. Their officers had hopes of grabbing the province for Queen Victoria.

Frémont moved to Sutter's Fort in June. While he waited for orders, a band of settlers started what later was called the Bear Flag revolt. Hoping to lure Mexican troops into battle, they stole one hundred seventy army horses. When General José Castro ignored the theft, they marched on Sonoma. There, General Guadalupe Vallejo surrendered without a fight. On June 14, the settlers raised a homemade flag. Under a bear and a red star, crude letters spelled out "California Republic."[1]

Events were moving swiftly. Frémont formed a

fighting unit called the California Battalion of Mounted Riflemen. With Kit leading the way, the 224 horsemen joined the settlers at Sonoma. United States naval forces under Commodore John Sloat took Monterey early in July. The Riflemen paraded through the streets a few days later. British officers came ashore to meet Kit. As one of them said, "Kit Carson is as well known [on the prairies] as the Duke [of Wellington] is in Europe."[2] The officers watched in awe as Kit showed off his marksmanship. He won some silver coins by hitting them from one hundred fifty yards.

Commodore Robert Stockton arrived to replace the elderly Sloat. By then General Castro and his men had moved south. Stockton marched Kit and his men onto a ship bound for San Diego. Kit was seasick most of the way. When he staggered off the ship, there was no fighting to be done. Castro had fled to Mexico.

The war appeared to be over. In September Frémont ordered Kit to carry a bundle of reports to Washington.

Kit's mission ended near Socorro, New Mexico. There he met General Stephen Kearny. Kearny was leading an army overland to California. He was outraged when Kit told him the fighting was over. To hasten his advance, he ordered Kit to serve as his guide. Because Kearny outranked Frémont, Kit had no choice. He gave the reports to another rider to carry eastward.

Two months later Kearny's advance force limped into California. The one hundred twenty men set up camp near Warner's Ranch, sixty miles northeast of San Diego. Word came that the Californios had retaken Los Angeles and Santa Barbara. Kearny sensed that this was his chance for glory.

On December 6, army scouts spotted Captain Andrés Pico and eighty horsemen near San Pasquale. Without consulting Kit, the headstrong Kearny ordered a charge. The Californios, who rode better horses, simply galloped away. Urged on by Kearny, the forty Americans chased them. Kit's horse stumbled, throwing him to the ground. He escaped being trampled, but his rifle was broken in the fall. He picked up a dead man's gun and mounted a stray horse.

By this time, Pico had sprung his trap. The Californios wheeled their horses and attacked. Caught by surprise, the soldiers fell under their sharp lances. The Californios did not break off the attack until Kearny's cannon arrived. By then thirty-six soldiers lay dead or wounded.

That night, the survivors huddled on a small hill. Mounted patrols cut off escape. Kearny sent Kit, Edward

Beale, and a young Native American to bring help. Kit led his small party across rocky, cactus-covered ground. The slightest noise could have meant discovery and death. Despite the sharp rocks and cactus spines, the men stuffed their moccasins into their belts. When they reached safety, the moccasins had fallen out. Barefoot, Kit and Beale limped through the canyons. Somehow, they reached San Diego. Stockton quickly sent a relief force to rescue Kearny and his men. At first doctors feared they might have to amputate Kit's bruised and bleeding feet. Luckily, the mountain man was a quick healer.

On December 29, Kearny and Stockton led their forces north. The Americans won a hard-fought victory at the Battle of Los Angeles. A few days later Andrés Pico found

Frémont at the Mission of San Fernando and surrendered. Kearny, who outranked Frémont, felt slighted. Kit did not worry about the argument. As far as he was concerned, the war was over.

John C. Frémont was a young army officer when he hired Kit Carson as his guide for an expedition to Oregon. The adventures the two men shared on the history-making trip forged a lifelong bond of friendship.

7

FROM DISPATCH RIDER TO SHEEPHERDER

Kit again headed east with dispatches in February 1847. During a brief stop in Taos, he caught up on some troubling news. The local tribe of Pueblo had risen in revolt. Governor Charles Bent had been scalped before army troops restored order. Josefa had escaped by dressing as a Pueblo.

Washington gave Kit a hero's welcome when he arrived in June. Reporters asked him about his exploits. People stopped him on the street to shake his hand. One dime novel cover showed him saving a woman from being scalped. Kit studied the drawing. "That thar may be true but I hain't got no recollection of it," he drawled.[1]

Frémont's wife, Jessie Benton Frémont, took Kit to the White House. The mountain man felt ill at ease in a new black suit. President James Polk listened carefully to his report. The president said Kit was a rare visitor, one who did not want a favor. Greatly impressed, Polk gave Kit an army commission as a second lieutenant. In June Lieutenant Carson headed west with new dispatches.

On reaching Monterey, Kit learned that the Kearny-Frémont feud had boiled over. Kearny had arrested Frémont. The court martial took place months later in the East. The court found Frémont guilty of refusing to obey orders. His pride injured, the Pathfinder resigned from the army.

Kit took command of a checkpoint at Tejon Pass, north of Los Angeles. His unit checked pack trains for smuggled goods and stolen horses. The job bored him. It was a relief

In 1847 Kit Carson returned to Taos to find that an attack by Native Americans had left the Pueblo Church in ruins. The raiders also scalped the governor. Kit's wife, Josefa, escaped a similar fate by dressing as a tribal woman.

General Stephen Kearny tried to seize command of U.S. forces when he reached California in 1846. John C. Frémont, caught in the power struggle, refused to take orders from Kearny. That refusal led to his arrest and court martial. As a lowly second lieutenant, Kit Carson was not involved in the conflict.

when he was sent east with headline-grabbing news. James Marshall had found gold at Sutter's Mill.

Lieutenant George Brewerton rode with Kit on that trip. Kit, he noted, used his saddle as a pillow. His half-cocked pistol always lay close at hand. He kept his rifle under his blanket to keep it dry. Brewerton also noticed that Kit stayed out of the firelight. Kit explained, "I don't want to have [a Native American] slip an arrow into me, when I can't see him."[2] If hostile warriors were lurking near, Kit built his usual nighttime cooking fire. Then he and his men slept at least a mile away.

Kit reached Washington in August. He was a hero to the public, but not to Congress. Senators who disliked Senator Benton, Fremont's father-in-law, refused to approve his commission. Kit's "crime" was his friendship with Frémont. His pleas for fair treatment of the Native Americans had cost him, too. To make matters worse,

Congress refused to pay him for his service in California. Kit refused to be bitter. As he put it, "I didn't do what I done for . . . pay. I done it for the United States."[3]

Kit returned to Josefa in October 1848. In the spring, he and Maxwell started a new ranch on Rayado Creek. Kit invested $2,000 in livestock, seeds, and supplies. Josefa stayed in town, where she gave birth to a son. Sadly, the baby died within the year. Kit turned a profit by selling his surplus horses and mules at Fort Laramie.

Josefa (Kit called her Little Jo) moved out to the ranch in the fall of 1850. Adaline, now fourteen, joined them the next spring. Kit loved his daughter, but could not control her. Two years later, Adaline married Louis Simmons, twenty years her senior. She died in California in 1860.[4]

The mountains were still Kit's first love. In the spring of 1852, he rounded up the Carson Men for one last, grand trapping trip. A year later, Kit and Maxwell bought six thousand five hundred sheep at fifty cents a head. The real test lay in keeping the sheep alive on the long trail to California. Kit followed the route he had pioneered with Frémont. Despite scrapes with Native Americans and wolves, the sheep reached Sacramento in good shape. A rancher paid $5.50 a head for the herd.

Kit spent a few days in San Francisco. The sleepy village had turned into a Gold Rush boomtown. By Christmas he was back in Taos. Kit was now forty-four years old. According to friends, he yearned for a quiet life with Josefa. If so, his wish did not come true.

8

PEACE AND WAR

In the 1850s, the Bureau of Indian Affairs carried on the government's business with Native Americans. The bureau sent agents to work with each tribe. Most of the agents came from the East and knew little about Native Americans. The bureau broke that pattern when it chose Kit as agent for the Ute, Pueblo, and Apache tribes. Kit understood Native American customs—and he was honest.

The Apache complained of missing food shipments. To feed themselves, they had been stealing livestock. Kit rode alone to meet with the band. The chiefs trusted him. They called off the raids when he promised they would be fed. Kit knew the truce was a shaky one. In a letter to the bureau, he wrote, "If you do not feed [the starving tribes], you cannot stop their raiding."[1]

Leaders of the Ute called on "Father Kit" at his home in Taos. As night fell, they smoked with him on his front porch. Baby William, born in 1852, played at Kit's feet.

Game was scarce, the chiefs would say. Where is our food? Again and again Kit wrote to plead for overdue shipments. At times he used his own money to feed hungry Native Americans.

By now Kit could sign his name. His reading and writing skills were more limited. The bureau would not pay for a clerk to write letters and keep books. It did pay for interpreters. Kit hired a young "interpreter" and assigned him to do clerical work. The fact that his "interpreter" spoke only English did not bother Kit.[2] He could talk to the Utes and Navajos in their own languages.

As an agent, Kit believed in fair play. If a white man harmed a Native American, Kit made sure the man was punished. If restless Native Americans broke the peace, he acted just as swiftly. The bureau's goal was to turn the

Kit and Josefa lived in this spacious home when they stayed in Taos. Visitors often saw Ute chiefs sitting near the door, waiting patiently to talk to "Father Kit." Today's visitors to Taos still flock to the house, which is now a museum.

tribes into peaceful farmers. Hearing that, Kit shook his head. The Navajo, he pointed out, raised corn and herded sheep. Even so, they often raided their neighbors. Only in battle, he explained, could a young man prove his manhood.

Kit spent as much time in Taos as he could. A daughter he named Teresina was born in 1855. A second son, Christopher, arrived in 1858. Kit liked to romp on the floor with the children. In 1860 his horse fell and dragged him down a mountain slope. He survived, but his painful chest injuries never fully healed.

In 1861 the Civil War broke out. Kit's loyalties lay firmly with the Union. In July he joined the New Mexico Volunteers. Lieutenant Colonel Carson stood firm when a Taos crowd tried to fly the Confederate flag. Before he raised the Stars and Stripes, he nailed the flag to its pole. He wanted to be sure no one could lower the flag.[3]

Southern troops entered New Mexico in 1862. Union forces, with Kit's eight companies among them, met the Texans at Valverde. Only Kit's men were holding their own when the bugle blew retreat. Three months later Kit took charge of a unit of the First New Mexico Cavalry. Unlike most officers, Kit told his men to call him by his first name. His troops lacked spit and polish, but they fought like tigers.

The army stripped its frontier forts of soldiers and sent them to fight in the East. With the soldiers gone, the Apache went back to looting wagon trains. Kit and his cavalry soldiers were called on to protect the settlers.

In his youth Kit Carson had served as a scout and guide. In his Canyon de Chelly campaign in 1864, he depended on men like Navajo scout Tom Tobin. The fringed buckskins Tobin wore for this portrait were saved for formal occasions. In the field the scout would have worn a more practical outfit.

Instead of shooting the raiders, Kit rounded them up. His success led to new orders. The Navajo had been attacking their ancient foes, the Hopi. Kit was told to bring peace to the region.

The Navajo were holed up in the rugged Canyon de Chelly (pronounced *de Shay*). Kit decided to starve them into making peace. He began his campaign by sealing off the canyon rim. Then he sent a strong force through the floor of the canyon. The troops did not pursue the fleeing Navajo up the rocky canyon walls. Instead, they burned fields and homes and cut down orchards. With their food supply destroyed, the Navajo surrendered. By mid-1864, Kit had settled nine thousand of them on a new reservation.

That fall, the Plains tribes went on a rampage. Kit was clearly the best choice to head up the government's response. The army sent him to fight the Kiowa and Comanche.

9

THE FINAL CONFLICTS

~~~~~~~~~~~~~~~

Kit led 335 soldiers and scouts into the Texas Panhandle in the fall of 1864. The plan called for him to link up with a second troop of cavalry. Together, they would attack the Kiowa camp on Palo Duro Creek. Near Adobe Walls, Kit and his men stumbled onto a large war party. As often happened, the Native Americans appeared where they were least expected.

Fire from Kit's two cannon beat back the first charge by the Kiowa. Quickly he ordered his men to fall back to the ruined fort at Adobe Walls. Within minutes several thousand Kiowa and Comanche warriors were circling the fort.[1] Kit saw that he had fallen into a trap. The warriors charged again and again. Each time a hail of rifle and cannon fire drove them back.

The Kiowa war chief then tried a new tactic. His men set a prairie fire they hoped would burn the soldiers out of the fort. Instead, the smoke gave Kit the cover he needed to stage a retreat. As he pulled back, his scouts lit a second fire. The wind-whipped flames drove the pursuing warriors away. By the time they circled back, Kit's column was out of reach.

The Kiowa were impressed. Kit had used their own hit-and-run methods. He had hurt them badly and escaped with light casualties. As a result, their leaders signed a peace treaty.

The Civil War ended in April 1865. By then Kit was a brigadier general. As a soldier, he guarded wagon trains. As a man trusted by the Native Americans, he helped write peace treaties. Kit also urged Congress to set up reservations far from towns and farms. The white man's liquor and diseases, he said, were destroying the tribes.[2]

Kit took up his final post in May 1866. Josefa and his five children joined him at Fort Garland, north of Taos. At fifty-six, Kit's health was failing. He could no longer ride a

Brigadier General Kit Carson posed for this portrait in 1866. His days as an Indian agent, Civil War officer, and conqueror of the Navaho lay behind him. He was still vigorous at age fifty-six, but injuries and illness were taking their toll.

A bronze statue in Kit Carson Memorial Park marks the final resting place of America's legendary mountain man. Kit and Josefa were buried here in Taos after both died in 1868. A modest man despite his achievements, Kit would have been amused to see himself cast in this heroic style.

horse. On his visits to the Ute, he traveled in a canvas bed slung between two mules. With miners pushing into their hunting grounds, the Indians were restless. It took all of Kit's skill to keep them at peace.

In November 1867, Kit resigned from the army. His hair had turned silver. He had trouble breathing. Even so, he agreed to escort a party of Ute east for treaty talks. The talks made good progress, but Kit was in great pain.

Doctors frowned when they saw the tumor in his throat. There was nothing they could do.

Kit made the long trip home to be with Josefa. In April 1868, she gave birth to a fourth daughter. Ten days later Josefa died of a fever. Her death robbed Kit of his will to live. The doctor at Fort Lyon put him on a liquid diet. Friends came by to read to him.

On May 23, Kit asked for "some fust-rate doin's." His nephew, Aloys Scheurich, grilled him a buffalo steak. Kit enjoyed the meat, coffee, and a final pipe. Then he coughed, and his mouth filled with blood. He called out, "I'm gone! Doctor, *compadre, adios!*"[3] A moment later the brave old mountain man's eyes closed in death.

A wagon carried Josefa and Kit home to Taos. They lie there today, in Kit Carson Memorial Park. Maps of the West show the wider impact of Kit's life. Carson, Colorado, and Carson City, Nevada, are named for him. So are Carson Pass and the Carson River. The federal building in Santa Fe provides a different memorial. Carved above the entrance is the simple tribute, "He led the way."

NOTES BY CHAPTER

Chapter 1

1. Thelma S. Guild and Harvey L. Carter, *Kit Carson: A Pattern for Heroes* (Lincoln, Neb.: University of Nebraska Press, 1984), pp. 120–121.

2. Bil Gilbert and the editors of Time-Life Books, *The Trailblazers* (Alexandria, Va.: Time-Life Books, 1973), p. 166.

3. Bernice Blackwelder, *Great Westerner: The Story of Kit Carson* (Caldwell, Idaho: Caxton, 1962), p. 138.

4. Shannon Garst, *Kit Carson, Trailblazer and Scout* (New York: Messner, 1942), p. 167.

5. DeWitt Peters, *The Life and Adventures of Kit Carson* (Freeport, N.Y.: Books for Libraries Press, 1970; original edition 1858), pp. 197–198.

Chapter 2

1. Thelma S. Guild and Harvey L. Carter, *Kit Carson: A Pattern for Heroes* (Lincoln, Neb.: University of Nebraska Press, 1984), p. 6.

2. Bernice Blackwelder, *Great Westerner: The Story of Kit Carson* (Caldwell, Idaho: Caxton, 1962), p. 15.

3. Bil Gilbert and the editors of Time-Life Books, *The Trailblazers* (Alexandria, Va.: Time-Life Books, 1973), p. 25.

4. Guild and Carter, p. 30.

Chapter 3

1. Thelma S. Guild and Harvey L. Carter, *Kit Carson: A Pattern for Heroes* (Lincoln, Neb.: University of Nebraska Press, 1984), pp. 34–35.

2. Ralph Moody, *Kit Carson and the Wild Frontier* (New York: Random House, 1955), p. 26.

3. Milo Milton Quaife, ed., *Kit Carson's Autobiography* (Lincoln, Neb.: University of Nebraska Press, 1966), p. 13.

4. DeWitt Peters, *The Life and Adventures of Kit Carson* (Freeport, N.Y.: Books for Libraries Press, 1970; original edition 1858), pp. 39–40.

5. Quaife, p. 21.

Chapter 4

1. Stanley Vestal, *Kit Carson, the Happy Warrior of the Old West* (Boston: Houghton Mifflin, 1928), p. 58.

2. Thelma S. Guild and Harvey L. Carter, *Kit Carson: A Pattern for Heroes* (Lincoln, Neb.: University of Nebraska Press, 1984), pp. 52–53.

3. Ibid., p. 63.

4. Vestal, p. 125.

5. Ibid., pp. 183–184.

Chapter 5

1. Thelma S. Guild and Harvey L. Carter, *Kit Carson: A Pattern for Heroes* (Lincoln, Neb.: University of Nebraska Press, 1984), pp. 97–99.

2. Stanley Vestal, *Kit Carson, the Happy Warrior of the Old West* (Boston: Houghton Mifflin, 1928), p. 194.

3. Ibid., p. 190.

4. John C. Frémont, *Memoirs of My Life* (Chicago: Bedford Clarke, 1887), p. 427.

5. Ralph Moody, *Kit Carson and the Wild Frontier* (New York: Random House, 1955), p. 120.

Chapter 6

1. Bernice Blackwelder, *Great Westerner: The Story of Kit Carson* (Caldwell, Idaho: Caxton, 1962), p. 171.

2. Thelma S. Guild and Harvey L. Carter, *Kit Carson: A Pattern for Heroes* (Lincoln, Neb.: University of Nebraska Press, 1984), p. 154.

Chapter 7

1. Bil Gilbert and the editors of Time-Life Books, *The Trailblazers* (Alexandria, Va.: Time-Life Books, 1973), p. 28.

2. George D. Brewerton, *Overland with Kit Carson* (New York: Coward, McCann, 1930), pp. 65–66.

3. Ralph Moody, *Kit Carson and the Wild Frontier* (New York: Random House, 1955), p. 134.

4. Thelma S. Guild and Harvey L. Carter, *Kit Carson: A Pattern for Heroes* (Lincoln, Neb.: University of Nebraska Press, 1984), p. 196.

Chapter 8

1. Ralph Moody, *Kit Carson and the Wild Frontier* (New York: Random House, 1955), p. 140.

2. Keith Wheeler and the editors of Time-Life Books, *The Scouts* (Alexandria, Va.: Time-Life Books, 1978), p. 32.

3. Bernice Blackwelder, *Great Westerner: The Story of Kit Carson* (Caldwell, Idaho: Caxton, 1962), p. 305.

Chapter 9

1. Ralph Moody, *Kit Carson and the Wild Frontier* (New York: Random House, 1955), p. 162.

2. Thelma S. Guild and Harvey L. Carter, *Kit Carson: A Pattern for Heroes* (Lincoln, Neb.: University of Nebraska Press, 1984), p. 210.

3. M. Morgan Estergreen, *Kit Carson: A Portrait in Courage* (Norman, Okla.: University of Oklahoma, 1962), p. 278.

GLOSSARY

apprentice—A trainee who learns a trade by working under the supervision of an experienced craftsperson.

bride price—A custom that requires a prospective husband to "buy" his wife-to-be by paying for her in money or goods.

Bureau of Indian Affairs—The government agency that tries to help Native Americans make the best use of their land and resources. The BIA also provides health, education, and welfare services.

cache—A hiding place. Mountain men often hid their furs in a cache rather than carry them from one camp to the next.

Californios—Landowners who ruled California in the years before the United States won control of the Mexican province.

cavalry—In the 1800s, an army unit trained to fight from horseback.

Civil War—The war between the North and the South, 1861–1865.

commission—A government document that appoints someone to a particular rank or office.

dime novels—Low-cost magazines that printed popular fiction during the late 1800s.

dispatch—An official message that the sender wants delivered as quickly as possible.

flint and steel—A fire-making device used in the 1800s. A mountain man started his campfire by striking sparks with his flint and steel.

greenhorn—Western slang for someone who is new to the region and unfamiliar with its customs.

Indian agent—In the 1800s, a government official who was responsible for keeping the peace and ensuring the well-being of a tribe of Native Americans.

interpreter—Someone who translates one language into a second language.

lodge—A wilderness dwelling, such as a wigwam or small log cabin.

mare—A female horse.

mission—A building or compound where priests educated Native Americans and converted them to Christianity.

moccasins—The soft leather shoes worn by Native Americans. Mountain men adopted moccasins as their standard footware.

mountain men—The fiercely independent hunters, explorers, and trappers who roamed the western mountain wilderness.

post—A permanent military camp or fort.

rendezvous—The meeting place where mountain men gathered each year to sell their furs, buy supplies, and socialize.

reservations—Large tracts of land set aside by the government for the use of Native American tribes.

scouts—Skilled woodsmen who helped guide expeditions through the wilderness.

stock—Domesticated animals, usually horses and cattle.

trail signs—The traces left by humans and animals as they move through a wilderness area.

trapper—Someone who makes a living by catching fur-bearing animals in traps.

MORE GOOD READING ABOUT
KIT CARSON

Blackwelder, Bernice. *Great Westerner: The Story of Kit Carson.* Caldwell, Idaho: Caxton, 1962.

Estergreen, M. Morgan. *Kit Carson: A Portrait in Courage.* Norman, Okla.: University of Oklahoma Press, 1962.

Guild, Thelma S., and Harvey L. Carter. *Kit Carson: A Pattern for Heroes.* Lincoln: University of Nebraska Press, 1984.

Moody, Ralph. *Kit Carson and the Wild Frontier.* New York: Random House, 1955.

Peters, DeWitt C. *The Life and Adventures of Kit Carson.* Freeport, N.Y.: Books for Libraries Press, 1970. Original edition 1858.

Quaife, Milo Milton, ed. *Kit Carson's Autobiography.* Lincoln, Neb.: University of Nebraska Press, 1966.

Vestal, Stanley. *Kit Carson, the Happy Warrior of the Old West.* Boston: Houghton Mifflin, 1928.

Wheeler, Keith, and the editors of Time-Life Books. *The Scouts.* Alexandria, Va.: Time-Life Books, 1978, pp. 24–33.

INDEX

¡B
CARSON

Sanford, William R.
  (William Reynolds).

Kit Carson.

90249

$14.95

DATE			